CYGNET & THOMASINA

Sailing Friends!

Written and Illustrated
by Anastasia Walsh

WindowDreams, Publisher

A WindowDreams Book
window.dream.art@gmail.com
Printed with Ingram Spark Publishing Group

Cygnet & Thomasina. Copyright © 2021 by WindowDreams
All rights reserved.

Library of Congress Cataloging-in-Publication
Data is available
ISBN 978-1-7363833-0-8 (print book)
eISBN 978-1-7363833-1-5 (digital book)

Book design by Anastasia Walsh
Editing by Rachel Korbin
Graphic Design Consultant Sydnea Lewis

Dedicated to Captain Ron, Captain Suzanne, and Captain Mark, whose true friendship inspired this story!

Time for bed.
Time for a story!

"Daddy! Tell us the story of the sailboat friends Thomasina and Cygnet again!" pleaded Duncan as he climbed up onto his bunkbed.

"No, silly," Betty argued from her room, which was right next to Duncan's.

"The story is called Cygnet and Thomasina!"

"Ahoy, my sweet mates," winked Daddy, making a joke, "maybe their names are Thoma-net and Cyg-sina!"

"No!!!" they screamed together, laughing on their beds in their own rooms.

"OK, little sailors," he said from the hallway outside their rooms, "climb under your covers and pretend they are the sails of your boats and you are sailing with Cygnet and Thomasina."

"Do you remember when we went out on Uncle Ron's sailboat, Cygnet?" asked Daddy. "Mommy was there too."

"Yeah, and I got to drive the boat!" Betty stated.

"Well, this is a story of Uncle Ron's sailboat and another sailboat, Thomasina, who were best friends. They had fun and they also took care of each other."

"How can boats be best friends? They can't talk and they can't send texts, so how can they?" demanded Betty.

"But it was true! I'll tell you about them," answered Daddy.

"Cygnet was a fast sailboat. He was built to win races.

Thomasina was a motor sailer. With her strong engine and sails, she could go on long trips."

"Sometimes Cygnet and Thomasina sailed close together and sometimes they were apart all day.

But most evenings they stayed near each other, and their captains met for dinner and played cards.

Cygnet had one captain—Uncle Ron.

And Thomasina had two captains—Mark and Suzanne."

"Every summer Thomasina and Cygnet sailed together to Snow Island in Maine.

Large birds called Ospreys had their nests on Snow Island.

In summertime, the Osprey chicks began learning how to fly.

The chicks would stand in their nests, excitedly flapping their wings to get strong."

"Sometimes they invited friends on board who enjoyed sailing—like us!

Did you know that one time Cygnet had a giraffe on board? Its head reached almost all the way up to the top of the mast!

The giraffe could see far ahead and helped Captain Ron to navigate!"

"And another time Thomasina had an elephant on the boat.

When its ears were spread out, it was like having another set of sails! When the wind was strong, Thomasina sailed faster than ever!

"Daddy..." frowned Betty, "how could an elephant fit on a sailboat?"

Daddy smiled. "Okay, I made that up. Isn't that a funny idea?"

Duncan and Betty rolled their eyes. Daddy could be pretty silly.

"Thomasina and Cygnet enjoyed easy sailing on most days. But once in a while there was a problem like when Cygnet got caught in the rope of a fishing net.

Luckily, Thomasina's Captain Suzanne was a scuba diver, so she dove under the boat to cut the rope off."

"Thomasina took care of Cygnet," Duncan whispered.

"She did, and Cygnet took care of her, too. Remember, they were best friends!" said Daddy.

Betty and Duncan nodded silently.

"One summer, Thomasina wasn't feeling particularly good. She got hot inside and tired easily. She just couldn't keep up with the other sailboats."

"Maybe she has the flu!" wondered Betty, who had been sick with the flu the week before.

"Sailboats don't get the flu," Duncan declared.

Betty stuck her tongue out at him, even though Duncan couldn't see her from his room.

"What could be wrong with Thomasina?" asked Daddy.

"Do you think she had a polar bear inside the bottom of her boat that was making her hot inside? Maybe the polar bear was hibernating!"

"No!!!" they yelled and laughed together.

"Or do you think she was towing a walrus family to their class reunion? And with so many big walruses, maybe the weight slowed her down?"

"No! Daddy, that's silly!" shrieked Betty.

"Stop Daddy, just tell the real story!" demanded Duncan, who was feeling a little sleepy.

"Okay," Daddy replied.

"Cygnet stayed nearby and watched Thomasina all day.

He wanted to make sure she was safe.

Every day Cygnet stayed with her, even when she was slow pulling into the harbor. And though it was late, their captains met for dinner and played cards."

"But one day when the wind was strong and the ocean current was fast, Cygnet forgot that Thomasina was sailing slow. Cygnet happily sped ahead.

Cygnet loved to feel the wind in his face as the sailboat raced across the water. The weather was cool, and the waves of the ocean were exciting! The big striped sail went up and Cygnet flew on the ocean!"

"But after a few hours he realized Thomasina wasn't with him. He couldn't see her near or far. 'Where was she? What was happening?' Cygnet wondered."

"I think Thomasina is lost!" shouted Duncan.

"Could she have gone the wrong way?" asked Daddy.

"Maybe…" Betty said in a nervous voice.

"Cygnet was terribly worried. Captain Ron called Thomasina's captains to find out where they were.

The captains told each other their positions from their GPS receivers."

"Thomasina was more than three hours behind Cygnet because the winds had slowed down and the ocean current had weakened. Thomasina was hot and tired and could only move forward slowly."

"Fortunately, Thomasina's captains were smart about how to bring Thomasina in for the night.

They gently guided her to a safe harbor in Pepperrell Cove."

"Thomasina thought she would have to spend the night alone.

Though she knew she was safe, she was still unhappy. Without her friends—especially Cygnet—she felt sad and lonely."

Betty and Duncan sank down in their pillows and looked sad;
they didn't want Thomasina to be lonely.

"Suddenly, Thomasina spotted a sailboat coming into the little harbor. It was Cygnet!"

"Yay!" exclaimed both children. "Hooray!"

"Cygnet circled around Thomasina until he found a place next to her to rest for the night.

And later, Cygnet and Thomasina's captains got together for the evening.

Of course, they had dinner and played cards."

"Is that the end of the story?" asked Betty.

"Not exactly," said her daddy.

The very next day, Thomasina headed up the river to the Boat Yard to have her engine replaced. It turned out that's why she was getting hot and tired—her engine wasn't working anymore."

"Did Cygnet have to sail by himself after that?" asked Duncan.

"Well, no—it was already the fall, and in New England that's when they lift sailboats out of the water anyway. They stay on land all winter to take a nice rest."

"But before that happened, Cygnet sang this to Thomasina:

> 'Dear friend of mine who sails so gracefully,
> You came through a hard time ever so courageously.'

And Thomasina answered:

> 'My handsome fella, such a smart sailor
> You stayed by my side when I was feeling paler.'

Then, together they crooned:

> 'Summer sailing days are pure love on the water
> Together we fly free as our friendship grows ever stronger!'"

Goodnight Betty!

Goodnight Duncan!

The End

Sailing Terms

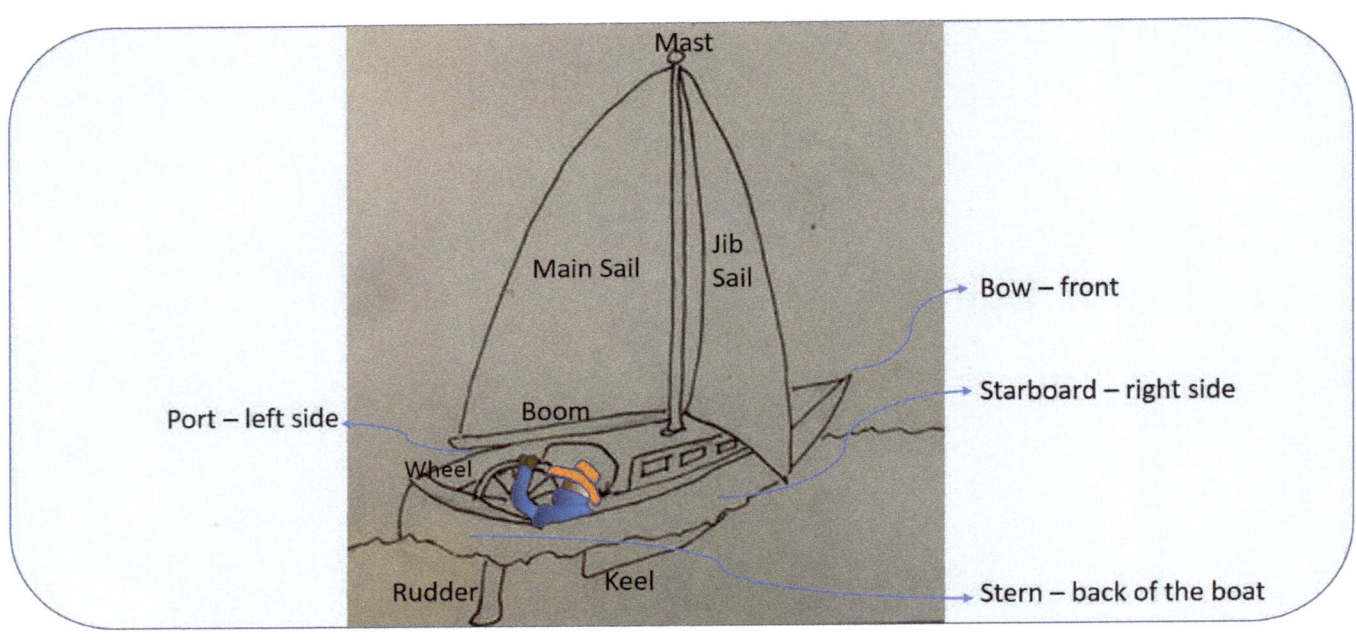

About the Author

Anastasia Walsh is an artist and novice sailor, residing in Maryland in the U.S. She hopes that Cygnet & Thomasina inspires children of all ages to learn to sail, or at least to dream of sailing!

CPSIA information can be obtained
at www.ICGtesting.com
Printed in the USA
BVHW021416040921
615856BV00003B/7